THE EFFECT OF A MENTORING AND EXTENDED LEARN
NORTH CAROLINA END OF COURSE TES

by

Portia Gibbs-Roseboro

A dissertation submitted to the faculty of
The University of North Carolina at Charlotte
in partial fulfillment of the requirements
for the degree of Doctor of Education in
Educational Leadership

Charlotte

2010

Approved by:

_____
Dr. Corey Lock

_____
Dr. Dawson Hancock

_____
Dr. Victor Cifarelli

UMI Number: 3422661

All rights reserved

INFORMATION TO ALL USERS
The quality of this reproduction is dependent upon the quality of the copy submitted.

In the unlikely event that the author did not send a complete manuscript
and there are missing pages, these will be noted. Also, if material had to be removed,
a note will indicate the deletion.

UMI®
Dissertation Publishing

UMI 3422661
Copyright 2010 by ProQuest LLC.
All rights reserved. This edition of the work is protected against
unauthorized copying under Title 17, United States Code.

ProQuest®

ProQuest LLC
789 East Eisenhower Parkway
P.O. Box 1346
Ann Arbor, MI 48106-1346

©2010
Portia Gibbs-Roseboro
ALL RIGHTS RESERVED

ABSTRACT

PORTIA GIBBS-ROSEBORO. The effect of a mentoring and extended learning program on North Carolina end-of-course Tests. (Under the direction of DR. COREY LOCK)

The purpose of this research study was to determine if effective interventions in the areas of mentoring and after school tutorial programs are put in place would increase Algebra I and English I students' academic performance on the end of course test. Specifically, the study addressed students who were currently three points below the passing scale score by the end of first semester based on their eighth grade end of grade test.

(1) Determine if assigning mentors the second semester of school was successful in assisting students in passing their Algebra I, and English I end of course test based.

(2) Determine if there is a significant difference between students who participated in the bubble program and students who did not.

The researcher used quantitative quasi experimental design. The sample population consisted of 232 students in the following subject areas: Algebra I and English I. The students involved in the Bubble program was established by an urban magnet high school in south eastern part of the United States. The researcher compiled data from the States' end of course Test results to determine whether or not there was a significant achievement difference between the two groups.

DEDICATION

This dissertation is dedicated to my parents, Ernest and Gwendolyn C. Gibbs, whose belief in me allowed me to reach this milestone in my life. It is also dedicated to my children who were patient and understanding during the long and tedious hours that kept me away from them as I completed this journey.

ACKNOWLEDGEMENTS

I would like to acknowledge Dr. Corey Lock, Dr. Dawson Hancock and Dr. Victor Cifarelli who believed that I could finish this project and never allowed me to stop.

TABLE OF CONTENTS

LIST OF TABLES	ix
CHAPTER 1: INTRODUCTION	1
Statement of the Problem	5
Defining Students of Academic Need/Research Questions	6
Definition of Key Terms	7
Significance of the Study	8
Organization of the Study	9
CHAPTER 2: LITERATURE REVIEW	10
Introduction/Purpose Statement/After School Programs Historical Importance	10
Communication	12
The After School Corporation (TASC) Study	14
Mentoring (Nurturing) and After School Programs/	15
Seattle Study	16
University of Illinois at Chicago Study	17
Middle School Study, Boston University	19
Evaluation of Afterschool Programs	20
Influences of After-School and Extended-Day Programs on Academics	20
"Self Efficacy" History and Effects on Academic Success	22
Mentoring: A Synthesis of P/PV's Research 1988 – 1995	24
Making a Difference in Schools	27
Making the Grade	29

CHAPTER 3: RESEARCH DESIGN AND METHODOLOGY	34
Introduction/Overview of Study's Methodology	34
Purpose Statement	37
Hypothesis/Null Hypothesis	39
Sample Selection	40
Meeting Student Needs	42
Instrumentation	43
Data Analysis	44
Limitations	45
Delimitations/Summary	46
Summary	47
CHAPTER 4: RESULTS	49
Introduction	49
Hypothesis/Null Hypothesis/Sample Description	51
Practice End-of-Course Results	54
Comparison for Practice test and End-of-Grade Results	55
CHAPTER 5: CONCLUSION	59
Research Questions	59
Summary of Findings	60
Discussion	61
Implications	64
Recommendations	66
REFERENCES	69

APPENDIX A: Sample Parent Letter	73
APPENDIX B: Sample Student Information	74
APPENDIX C: Sample Student Information Card	75

LIST OF TABLES

TABLE 1: Sample Demographic	52
TABLE 2: Sample Demographic Ethnicity	53
TABLE 3: Practice Test Mean Results for Algebra I and English I	54
TABLE 4: Post-Test Mean Results for Algebra I and English I	57
TABLE 5: Growth Mean Results for English I	57
TABLE 6: Growth Mean Results for Algebra I	58

CHAPTER 1: INTRODUCTION

"When children succeed, the teacher succeeds. When the teacher succeeds, the world succeeds. When the world succeeds, we find peace. Where we find peace, we find love, all things are possible" (Collins, 1992, p. 89).

In a time when high stakes testing often determines whether students succeed at school, it is important for educators to do what they can to assist students and ensure success. Throughout the history of schooling, administrators and educators have attempted many interventions in an effort to assist students in achieving academic excellence in school (Alexander, 2000). Many educational leaders in today's schools struggle with providing appropriate academic support for their students. Issues such as lack of parental involvement and lack of appropriate afterschool programs very often contribute to students' lack of academic success in school (Posner, 1999). As a result, it is important that appropriate guidance and extended day programs are implemented that can enable students to achieve their academic goals (Scott-Little, 2002). Currently, extended day tutorial and mentorship programs whose primary focus is on kindergarten through eighth grade students are in place and are provided through the both in and out of school personnel.

State and national standards require students to pass rigorous standardized tests and state exams. Because of the emphasis placed on these standardized examinations, whether students' academic progress can be improved by mentoring and after school tutoring is important to educational leaders across the nation (After School Alliance, 2002). Nationally, students are constantly pressured about their ability to pass mathematics tests in order to be competitive worldwide (Thompson, 2001). Students no longer compete merely nationally but internationally as well in both the job market and institutions of higher education. Educational leaders such as teachers and administrators must understand the importance of providing children with every opportunity to enter into the competition with a competitive knowledge base. In order to prepare students, educational leaders must eliminate as many obstacles as possible that may hinder success and also provide opportunities such as guidance during and after school, remediation opportunities, and remedial tools (Posner, 1999). Educational leaders can only do this by analyzing test data which help determine where their students are on quarterly, semester, and yearly bases and by making decisions that will assist current and future students in their schools (Baker, 2000).

Since all students are required to pass their end of course tests as mandated by the state, it is important to assist students in successfully obtaining test-taking skills. One of the most critical areas for students is mathematics, an area in which many minority students struggle. Mathematics is also a requirement for college acceptance, and because one of the goals at the high school level is that students are accepted into higher education institutions, the school must ensure that students are able to successfully complete mathematics requirements (Schwartz, 2002). Students are also required to successfully complete and pass English I end of course test, which is one of four English requirements for graduation. In order to effectively assist students in schools, educational leaders must be able to correctly identify students with a specific academic need. Once students in need are identified, then schools must correctly identify key personnel within the school to assist (mentor) the now identified students. Each step in recognizing students in need of academic support is a step toward successfully helping students in their pursuit of a high school diploma and higher education opportunities.

High schools in the state of North Carolina are currently under attack by both state and local officials (Archer, 2006). In particular, the Leandro Case in North Carolina has determined that high schools are failing their students and something must be done to assist high schools in North Carolina (Archer, 2006). The Leandro case initially began as a law suit against poorer districts in the state to provide equal education for all students. Other districts joined in the lawsuit and Judge Howard Manning pointed out that schools are failing low income, minority, and limited English proficient students frequently called "at-risk" students. Many North Carolina children are not receiving the sound basic education to which they are entitled. The right to a sound basic education extends to all children, but is especially crucial for children "at-risk" of academic failure in school (e.g. those who come from low income, single parent, or non-English speaking homes). In addition, students who drop out of school are not receiving a sound basic education. If necessary, the state must provide additional services and funds to help all North Carolina Children and youth meet the Leandro standard. (North Carolina Child Advocacy Institute, 2005, p. #)

In addition, given the high stakes testing in North Carolina, students must be prepared to pass their end of course tests. To ensure students are successful in their pursuits, educational leaders must put strategies such as mentoring and extended learning opportunities in place (Schwartz, 2005). It is also essential for educational leaders to understand the importance of meeting adequate yearly progress (AYP) as established by the No Child Left Behind Act 2003 (NCLB). Such progress markers are no longer crucial for students' success alone but also for the success of the school and for the school district as well. No longer are students' academic performances at stake but also the schools ability to stay functioning at the appropriate level according to the Federal Government and NCLB.

Because high schools are under attack from the media and education professionals such as the federal government (NCLB, 2003) for not providing the necessary services required to meet students' needs (Crosby, 1999; Landson-Billings, 2001; Navarro, 1999), it is important that educational leaders actively seek strategies such as teacher mentors within the school, extended day tutorials, and after school tutorials to better assist students' academic progress. High school students seem to have problems transitioning from middle grades and are disconnected because of the major shift from a child-centered environment in middle school to a more independent, self-sufficient environment in high school (Darling-Hammond, 1997). Therefore, researchers like Cole et. al (2001), Darling-Hammond (1997), and Landson-Billings (2001) have investigated smaller learning communities and nurturing (mentoring) to make the transition from middle school to high school seamless for students. In their writings they have found that a compilation of mentoring, smaller learning communities actually allow students for better preparedness in school. Other issues facing high school students are the size of the school and the inability to make the environment more personal for students (Tatum, 1999).

This case demonstrates the ongoing problems in high schools across the state and across the nation and demonstrates the need for researchers to take a closer look at how high school students are assisted in the completion of their formal education.

Statement of the Problem

This study examined the impact of after school extended learning opportunities and mentors on students end of course test in Algebra I, and English I. The current study determined the effectiveness of interventions for high school students in urban high schools not only in North Carolina but also across the nation. Researchers have focused on the effects of mentoring and extended learning from pre-kindergarten to eighth grade; however, very few have reported on interventions at the high school level (After School Alliance, 2002). Critics of high schools are demanding better achievement results and are accusing school systems of educational genocide but they have not offered any sound suggestions for funding to fix the problem (Archer, 2006). Despite this observed trend, the school studied in this dissertation established interventions to improve academic achievement for freshmen students enrolled in Algebra I and English I, which are listed below:

1. Assigned mentors to students during the second semester of school to assist students in passing their Algebra I and English I end of course tests.
2. Provided academic and behavior contracts.
3. Provided opportunities for academic enrichment through extended learning and computer tutorial.

Defining Students of Academic Need

The high school studied identified students who, based upon their third quarter test scores, had the potential to pass the end of course test with interventions. The majority of participants in the present study were ninth graders. Therefore, many students from the school studied in the present study here either two points below the passing scale score or just three points above the scale score by the end of first semester. This group became the focus group identified and named as students "on the bubble."

The following interventions were put in place, which will be explained further in subsequent sections: Core Academy, Extended Day, Academic/Behavior Contract, a teacher mentor, and academic performance teams. These interventions were selected based on research which showed gains for students who had both academic and behavior problems that improved when involved with a mentor and extended learning hours (Kulger, 2001). The administration and staff believed that these interventions would allow students to successfully pass their end of course tests in Algebra I and English I. The control group consisted of students not receiving the interventions.

Research Questions

1. What were the reported changes in the End of Grade test in Algebra I and English I for the students who participated in the mentoring and extended learning program over the second semester?

2. Was there a significant difference in the growth End of Grade test scores in Algebra I and English I for those students in a regular education program who

participated in Extended Learning Program as opposed to those who did not participate in a mentoring and extended learning program?

Definition of Key Terms

The definitions of the Key terms used in this study are as follows:

A. Formal Definitions

1. *Mentor* – Teacher within the school who will make continuous contact with identified students.
2. *Pre-Requisite Course* – course required before admittance into Algebra I, and English I.
3. *No Child Left Behind Act 200120 U.S. § § 6301-7941 (NCLB, 2001)* – Federal program which provides accountability for schools, implemented by the Bush Administration.
4. *PLATO* – Computer based program designed to improve students' basic skills in mathematics with approximately 50 minutes per day in the computer lab.

B. Operational Definitions

1. *Bubble Students* – Students who had the potential to either increase or decrease their chances of passing the Algebra I, Biology, English I, and Geometry End of Course Test based on their previous scale score in prerequisite courses, teacher recommendation, and first and second quarter exams.
2. *Bubble Program* – Identified the group of students who were assigned mentors and participate in the extended learning proram.
3. *Core Academy* – An after school remediation class to assist students with academics from first semester in Algebra I, Biology, English I and Geometry.

4. *Extended Day Tutorial* – A program that assisted students in Algebra I, Biology, English I, and Geometry who struggle with understanding specific concepts related to Geometry.

5. *After-school Tutorial* – A tutorial program, which allows students to practice remedial skills independently using the PLATO computer program.

6. *After School Programs* – Programs offered after school hours that are extended day programs connected to the curriculum taught during the regular school day.

7. *Parental Contact* – Notification to parents about their student's involvement in the bubble program.

Significance of the Study

The present study examined extended learning, attendance, and behavior barriers to academic success and called for an individualized approach to assist high school students in their academic pursuits that may be beneficial in schools outside of the one utilized in the completion of this research.

Because change happens when schools allow all students the opportunity to succeed, it is important for educational leaders to work within their current school settings by applying the necessary approaches to yield favorable outcomes (Collins, 2000). The present research has the potential to expand far beyond one high school and to assist students nationally through programs that utilize faculty and staff within the school building.

Organization of the Study

Following Chapter One, which discusses an overview of the study and its purpose, Chapter Two is a review of literature of previous research related to the major constructs that support student achievement in relation to mentors, during and after school tutorials. Chapter Three details the study's methodology, including the study's research design and hypotheses, population and sample, instrumentation, data collection procedures and data analysis procedures. Chapter Four reports the findings in the study in terms of its specific research questions and hypotheses. Chapter Five include discussion of findings, conclusions of results and the implication of the study for both further research and future practice in educational leadership.

CHAPTER 2: REVIEW OF LITERATURE

Introduction

This study was designed to determine if there were significant achievement differences between two groups of students. One group of students participated in an extended day program after school for two hours twice a week and was assigned a mentor. The second group of students did not participate in the extended day program, and they were not assigned mentors. This chapter is a review of literature pertaining to this study. The following major topics are discussed: urban schools, standardized testing, theories of learning, remediation, funding, the No Child Left Behind Act of 2003, and mentoring.

Purpose Statement

The purpose of this literature review was to: (1) present past and recent studies that reviewed on afterschool programs, (2) discuss elements that contributed to prior programs' success, (3) provide the importance of mentoring and nurturing in afterschool programs to student academic gains (4) discuss funding issues of afterschool programs and finally (5) discuss the influence afterschool programs have had on academics.

After School Programs Historical Importance

There has always been an emphasis placed upon the separation of achieving between the sexes; however, with the increasing issues of crime and delinquency among girls, the focus turned to monitoring children during the period of "risk and opportunity." Once idle students were monitored, the issue became what learning experiences the afterschool programs accomplished. Afterschool programs began to do what schools could not during the school day and the "learning by doing" principle, promoted by the progressivist John Dewey, was implemented. (Halpern, 2002). This principle entailed an experimental method which unites mental activity and experience, and allowed for the creation of new knowledge.

During the World War II era, the rise of latchkey children led existing afterschool programs to assume more explicit child-care functions. With the identification of latchkey children emerged nurseries, day cares, and other supplemental programs that assisted working parents with raising their children (Halpern, 2002). During this time organizations such as the Boys and Girls Club, YMCA, and YWCA were restructured and continued to assist parents with childcare. Later in the 1990's afterschool programs began to focus on becoming extensions of the school day and not working in isolation. Miller and Marx (1990) described after school programs as "unsupervised play and [wastes] of time," leading cities such as New York to argue that these programs should "make every minute meaningful," a slogan created by The National Governors' Association (1999). Thus, came a shift of after school programs to promote academic achievement. Halpern (2002) asserted that "after school programs can serve as a developmental resource and support for children only to the extent that they are allowed to work from a modest and reasonable story line. And, they can fulfill some of their potential if they themselves are adequately nurtured, supported, and protected."

Furthermore, Halpern connects the importance of nurturing students and making the adult connection between students during afterschool programs. Since the inception of afterschool programs, safety and security have been underlying themes (Halpern, 2002), and these goals are only achieved when the relationship between the adult and student is strong.

Communication

"It [a system of free common schools] knows no distinction of rich and poor of bond and free, or between those, who in the imperfect light of this world, are seeking, through different avenues, to reach the gate of heaven. Without money and without price, it throws open its doors, and spreads the table of its bounty for all the children of the State." (Mann, 1968, p. 754)

This statement is a reflection of what public education initially stood for in our society. However, with the ever-changing purpose of schooling today, educators are faced with the enormous task of defining school's purpose and ensuring children are prepared for the world of high stakes testing and international competitiveness (NCLB, 2003). Therefore, curriculum planners and teachers must be acquainted not only with their immediate educational programs, but they must also be informed of what takes place at each school level (elementary, middle, high school and collegiate). This can allow teachers to better understand their students' needs based on their prior educational experiences, which would allow teachers to assess their students much earlier in the school year and provide for more individualized instruction. Knowledge of various educational programs can also allow teachers to provide more continuity of instruction for after school programs which can enhance the students' learning process. This continuity is important when determining how best to continue instruction in extended learning programs (After School Alliance, 2002).

To provide the optimum learning experience during extended hours, teachers must equip themselves with information about students' learning experiences during the school day. This happens through effective communication among educational professionals within the school building. Senge (2000) noted, it is "incumbent among educational leaders to remove the bureaucratic web that hinders continuous communication flow throughout the organization" (p. 232). Schools must establish a cyclical flow of communication within their buildings to allow for effective communication to continue even during extended school hours. Senge (2000) also asserted that this cyclical flow is only successful when individuals participating in the process are confident enough to make decisions independent of principals and administrators, thus providing more confident and committed teachers. This only happens when the school allows teachers to collaborate as professionals and make decisions that are in the best interest of the student in the absence of the bureaucratic web that often hinders academic opportunities for students. Professional collaboration is vital to academic success because it keeps an open line of communication among all of the stakeholders involved within the school (Senge, 2000). Senge (2000) also points out the importance of providing sufficient professional development for educators to make certain they are able to complete the education process independently. Therefore, it becomes important for teachers to determine the type of instruction, curriculum, and meaning of instruction for students in extended learning programs.

Regular school day teachers must communicate with extended learning teachers regarding the type of instructional delivery they must communicate regarding the instructional methods they use in a variety of subjects within their classroom in order to make after school instruction relevant to students' in class learning experience (Hankes, 1996). To enhance the student's learning experience, after school instruction must be relevant to classroom instruction. Wink (2001) noted that if learning is not meaningful to students, what the teacher does is irrelevant. But the most important meaning is from students' learning experiences that are must be relevant to what is happening in their classrooms during the regular school day as well as in the after school program (Alexander, 2000). Therefore, teachers must have a firm understanding of what students are experiencing in their regular classrooms. This understanding is facilitated by effective communication.

Promoting Learning and School Attendance Through After-School Programs

The After-School Corporation (TASC) Study

The After-School Corporation conducted a three-year study of students in New York City and throughout the state of New York who participated in the TASC program. The study concentrated on the type of students in after school programs, patterns of after school participation, the effects of achievement overall, afterschool attendance and characteristics of students who derive benefits from TASC. The evaluation of the program was significant to continued funding for students in afterschool programs.

The participants in the TASC project included students that demonstrated high levels of educational risk, defined by existence of poverty, baseline achievement, status as English Language Learners, recent immigrants, racial/ethnic minority group members, and recipients of special education. The median participation increased over the three-year period. In the 1998 school year, students attended the TASC project for a median of eighty days. The time increased to a median of ninety-nine days during the 1999 school year, and ultimately reached a median of 109 days in the 2000-01 school year. According to TASC, this increase in student participation indicated that students and their families matured or that the school administration made more efforts to promote higher attendance over the three-year period. Students identified in the project gained six scale-score points more than similar non-participants after only two years of participation in the program. The study also found that Blacks, Hispanics, and Special Education students demonstrated increases in their academic performance as a result of their participation in the TASC project. In addition, the students who participated in the project increased their overall school attendance compared to non-participants whose attendance did not show a significant difference at each grade level (TASC, 2002).

The outcome of the program evaluation was that after school attendance rates improved, which meant that participating students experienced increasing levels of exposure to TASC activities. Participation in the program also increased mathematics achievement across grade levels and types of students. The third finding from the program evaluation was that students who were at greatest academic risk appeared to have received the greatest benefit from regular TASC participation. Finally the TASC project participation impacted school attendance through significant gains.

Mentoring (Nurturing) and After School Programs

Shumow's (2001) research indicated that children from high-risk backgrounds have both the most to gain from after school programs, but also the least access to such programs. However, Shumow (2001) also states that afterschool programs can only benefit those who are willing to participate. He suggests this can be done through a positive emotional climate in the afterschool program. He also reminds educators that success in afterschool programs does not come by extending the regular school with traditional classroom lesson and routines, but by providing activities related to their classroom experience.

Seattle Study

Seattle, Washington created the first state remediation assistance program. It was designed to assist the Federal Compensatory Education Programs. Funds from the Compensatory Education Program were directed toward states that offered programs geared toward basic skills and remediation. The funding was provided for grades two through six. The funds were in place for two years; however the funding was combined with remediation funds which left minimal funding for programs when funded separately.

In September of 1983, courts passed a judgment that directed funding for only their remediation assistance program and separate funding was provided for grades 2 through 6, beginning in the 1984–1985 school year. As a result of reduced funding, the school district joined other districts within the state of Washington that sued for additional funding to support their remediation program (Rasp & Macquarrie, 1987). There was significant growth for the students during the year of the remediation program's implementation, in the areas of mathematics, reading, and language (Rasp & Macquarrie, 1987).

University of Illinois at Chicago Study

This was a study conducted on the assessment of afterschool programs as contexts for youth development. The study provided an assessment method that enabled evaluation of varied youth programs in accordance with the student's development agenda. The study includes 125 African-American students in grades six through ten, as well as samples of students who participated in other afterschool programs. The analysis of the survey data indicated that only some afterschool programs provided more opportunities and supports for youth development than students receive during the school day but that almost all provide significantly more attractive activities (Khane, 421). The most significant difference was for African-American male students. The study compared community and school-based after school programs and found that school-based after school programs were more effective for students academic growth.

The study indicated benefits of structured after school programs and indicated that many of the programs emphasized the value of safe structured and enjoyable opportunities. The researchers also indicated offering activities that were not available during the regular school day as an asset of afterschool programs. Another positive attribute of afterschool programs is the ability of the program to focus on developmental goals of youth and not solely concentrate on academic goals. The developmental goals allowed for relationships to occur between caring and supportive adults, which provided motivation, high expectations and mentoring for youth (Khane, 2002). This was significant for the researcher based on studies sample group were African American. In the Illinois study African American boys felt disconnected from their schools (Khane,

2002). The study further indicated that the relationships established between youth and staff professionals of after school programs can facilitate person support and monitoring.

The study presented concerns regarding afterschool programs of supervised care but were not of high quality. In such after school programs often the connections to academic content were weak, skill development was not systematic, youth capacities were not fully engaged and long term relationships between adults and youth frequently are not developed (Khane, 2002).

The need for quantitative indicators of afterschool programs is needed; however, the ease and accuracy of assessments are limited by various factors. One factor is the inability to collect appropriate data because of the brevity of many programs and youth often participate in multiple programs simultaneously, therefore creating difficulty to determine which program is actually causing the student's improvement. The second is that various outcomes for the program are not specified and are often unclear. In addition participation is voluntary, which makes comparisons to non-participants and causality difficult. Finally, the program's quality care be heavily dependent upon particular features of the curriculum, implementation, and the leader of the after school activity or program.

The study concluded that the quality of after school programming was uneven. Because of inequity in the after school programs the study also indicated that African American boys did not have the maximum benefit of the after school program and in particular did not feel the necessary support within many of the programs. There was strong evidence that linked student perceptions of social support to academic achievement; therefore, the researchers indicated that further investigation is needed to determine which programs have desirable contexts and explore how these practices can be incorporated in the regular school day.

Middle School Study, Boston University

Shann (2001) conducted a study in four inner city schools on how students spend their time after school and on weekends. The schools in the study surveyed a population that consisted of 90% of students who were economically disadvantaged and were minority youth. The study indicated that many of the students participated in events after school which did not incorporate structured academic activities. Students elected to participate in activities that involved hanging out with friends, watching television and one-third did not do any reading after school. However, surveys of the students' teachers indicated teachers were reluctant to send students home with textbooks. Due to funding issues with textbooks, many teachers sent worksheets, and assignments in their notebooks as a replacement.

Shann's (2001) study also emphasized the importance of meaningful adult relationships with minority students. She mentions the importance of the relationship between adults and youth are strong. In addition to the relationship, the adult and the student must be involved in activities that are engaging and positive. Shann presented that this could be done through afterschool programs. Such programs that "offer a combination of academic, cultural, recreational and life skill activities for students, can provide a welcoming, safe and educational oasis in the barren desert of after school hours." (Shann, 2001)

Evaluations of After School Programs

The availability of funds for afterschool programs has increased according to the evaluation research conducted by Scott-Little, Hamann, and Jurs (2002). Their research indicated that there was difficulty in conducting evaluations on afterschool programs through meta-evaluation because of limited use of research designs that support causal conclusions and insufficient information to allow for meta-analysis of program effects. However, the researchers did suggest that their overall findings appear to support afterschool programs, because the programs have a positive impact on participants. They also suggested that more rigorous research designs were necessary to provide data that clearly document program effects.

Influences of After-School and Extended-Day Programs on Academics

A 1998 study conducted by Frazier and Morrison measured the relationship between extended instructional time and cognitive and psychosocial development of ninety kindergarten students in four magnet schools and ninety-one kindergartners in one extended-year school. The city's population was approximately 185, 000 of which 36% were African American. This study added thirty instructional days to the 180 day school calendar. Data for the study were gathered through parent questionnaires, student achievement tests, through performance perception instruments, and observations done of kindergarten classrooms. Results from the study indicated participants of the extended year program out-performed the traditional students on cognitive competence rating from kindergarten to first grade. However there was not a significant difference between the two groups on peer acceptance and physical competence.

Posner and Vandell conducted a study in 1999 with a group of third grade students from nine Milwaukee elementary schools who they followed for two and one-half years. The groups studied were from low-income students from both African-American and White student households. The study attempted to show the amount of time spent during after school hours affected the adjustment to fifth grade. Demographics information was collected through questionnaires, and times-use interviews were collected from telephone interviews with each child periodically throughout the two-and-a-half year study. The students' academic records were obtained from all participating schools. Teachers completed a rating for children's work habits and emotional well-being in the third and fifth grades. The results indicated that students who attended after- school programs spent more time on academic and extracurricular activities. However students who were involved in informal afterschool care spent most of their time on unstructured non-academic activities. Posner and Vandell (1999) concluded that children's after-school activities were related to their academic performance and emotional adjustment.

This chapter has included a review of literature, which generally indicates that students who spend their after-school time in organized, academic extended-day programs exhibit positive achievement effects on end of course tests. The review of literature also indicates that nurturing is needed in secondary education to increase students' level of interest in school and afterschool programs. These effects may be observed in students having fewer discipline problems, improvement in academic performance, increased work and study habits, and increased school attendance.

"Self Efficacy" History and Effects on Academic Success

Pajares' (1996) study provided a background for looking at the role of self-efficacy and school achievement. In this study Pajares elaborates on Bandura's social cognitive theory. Albert Bandura's social cognitive theory is summarized as "self-referent thought mediates between knowledge and action and through self-reflection individuals evaluate their own experiences and thought processes". (Bandura, 1986) Pajares continues to discuss Bandura's social cognitive theory through Bandura's "reciprocal determinism, the view that (a) personal factors in the form of cognition, affect and biological events (b) behavior, and (c) environmental influences create interactions that result in a triadic reciprocality."(Bandura, 1986) Pajares also provides Badura's definition of self-efficacy which is, "beliefs in one's capabilities to organize and execute the course of action required to manage prospective situations". (Bandura, 1986) Indicating that people who believe a task is either difficult or easy will determine the student's willingness to complete the task at hand, or increase/decrease levels of motivation. The construct of self-efficacy has only been around since 1977, however it has been tested and received support from various disciplines in and out of the field of education. Bandura did caution researchers attempting to predict students' academic outcomes by only utilizing self-efficacy beliefs. He states "...self-efficacy beliefs should be assessed at the optimal level of specificity that correspond to the criterial task being assess and the domain of the functioning being analyzed." (Bandura, 1986) Unfortunately Bandura's caution has gone unheeded by educational researchers, which has resulted in generalized capabilities having little or no relevance to criteria task with which they are being compared.

Though researchers have reported that self-efficacy beliefs are correlated to academic choices, changes and achievement, the correlation is weak between self-efficacy and the individual student's ability to perform on various assessments. Studies have indicated that students with high self-efficacy demonstrate a greater academic persistence than students with low self-efficacy. The higher efficacy is necessary to maintain high academic achievement. Studies that report a lack of relationship between self efficacy and performance often suffer from problems either in specificity or correspondence. A regression model with math anxiety, the quantitative score on the American College Test (ACT-Q), and prior math experience revealed that self-efficacy did not account for a significant portion of the variance in math performance. Researchers have also found that self-efficacy though weak predictor, was a better indicator for mathematics than any other discipline.

The implications of self-efficacy in research analysis indicate that there is only a small impact on a student's belief of success and the student's actual success. In the study currently completed "Mathematics self-efficacy and mathematical problem solving implications using vary forms of assessment" it has been concluded that for a self-efficacy instrument to be accurate it must be similar to the future assessment. In mathematics self-efficacy instruments the questions asked are general and not specific to the types of problems being used on the actual assessment. However there is a caution made by the researchers not to provide the exact items on the assessment on the self-efficacy instrument, due to the bias which would be caused by correlated specifics. Researchers Pajares and Miller suggest for self-efficacy instruments to be a predictor of academic success that instrument must be content specific and not measure generalized ability. Pajares and Miller go on to discuss that though self-efficacy did not play a significant role in the student achievement as a whole, there was a difference in boys and girls self-efficacy perceptions.

Mentoring: A Synthesis of P/PV's Research 1988 - 1995

Sipe (1996) conducted a research synthesis of mentoring through public/private ventures. Sipe posed five questions in his research analysis. 1) Can participating in mentoring programs make important and observable changes in the attitudes and behaviors of at-risk youth? 2) Are there specific practices that characterize effective mentoring relationships? 3) What program structures and supports are needed to maximize "best practices" among mentors? 4) Can mentoring be integrated into large-scale youth-serving institutions? 5) Are there large numbers of adults with enough flexible time and emotional resources to take on the demands of mentoring at-risk youth? Sipes answered the questions by reviewing ten research reports, which included what many refer to as the 1995 landmark impact study on mentoring Big Brothers Big Sisters Study (Cannata, Graringer, MacRae, Wakeland, 2005).

The first question posed by Sipe was: Can participating in mentoring programs make important and observable changes in the attitudes and behaviors of at-risk youth? Sipe (1996) answered this question by providing the history of Big Brothers Big Sisters (BBBS) mentoring program. BBBS has a well established program that has been around working collectively with boys and girls since 1977 (Sipe, 1996). The organization was founded by Ernest Coulter, a judge, in 1904 by getting volunteers to work with the increasing number of boys he was beginning to see in his courtroom. By 1916 the volunteer program was effectively running in 96 cities. In 1977 the Big Brothers added to its organization Big Sisters and began to work with young girls as well as boys.

Big Brothers Big Sisters is also the only program with sufficient numbers to be included in the research (Sipe, 1996). This impact study provided definitive evidence that youth can obtain benefits through participating in a well-run mentoring program. The study found that you who participated in the program received slightly better grades, less drug use, better behavior and attendance in school for the length of the study. Due to the age constraints of 10 – 15 year old youth Sipe (1996) pointed out that the study cannot be generalized to either younger or older youth.

For question two Sipe (1996) asked if there were specific characteristics for effective mentoring relationships. Sipe (1996) reported the key to a successful mentor mentee relationship depends on the mentor being able to involve the youth in deciding how they will spend their time, make a commitment to being consistent and dependable, patient, allow youth to have fun, respect youth's view point and the mentee must also be able to seek advice from program staff as necessary. Less effective mentors try to transform or reform the youth by setting goals and tasks too soon. They also emphasized behavior change more than mutual trust and respect. Mentors do not meet with youth on a regular basis and attempt to instill values that are not a part of the youth's home life is not an effective strategy for mentors. Additionally they did not actively seek involvement form the Big Brothers staff.

Third Sipe asked what program structures and supports are needed to maximize "best practices among mentors?" Sipe (1996) answers this by providing a description of appropriate screening, orientation and training of mentors. A screening suggestion offered by Sipe is to review the volunteers' life commitments and discuss how they intend to fit their mentoring responsibilities into their overall schedules. This was done to insure that the mentor is able to meet regularly with their mentee. During this screening process those who were unable to meet regularly should be screened out of the process. For orientation and training Sipe (1996) states that there has not been a consistent training program for mentors, however she does note the importance of providing a guide for mentors. However when experienced mentors were surveyed they thought that experience was the best teacher. To obtain continuous success ongoing support and supervision in addition to appropriately matching mentor and mentee are also key characteristics to a successful mentoring program.

Questions four and five seek to address how to assist youth through a large scale institutional process of mentoring and the availability of adults to participate in the mentoring programs. At the time Sipe conducted the study the only group that could be addressed were youth who were in the juvenile justice system. Sipe (1996) was able to address the scale question by directly examining the recruitment practices of all the programs studied. Sipes (1996) states there are an overwhelming number of mentees requesting mentors and there are not enough mentors. This is the challenge when attempting to integrate mentoring into a large-scale youth serving institutions. As asked in question five, "Are there large numbers of adults with enough flexible time and emotional resources to take on the demands of mentoring at-risk youth?" Limitations such as funding to recruit volunteers on a large scale tend to hinder recruitment efforts. Even if mentoring programs were able to recruit on a large scale the screening of mentors is a long process and many would withdraw from the program or they would not clear their background checks.

Making a Difference in Schools

A school-based mentoring impact study conducted by the Big Brothers Big Sisters identified nine findings of how mentoring youth affects their school performance (Herrera, Grossman Baldwin, Kauh, Feldman, & McMaken, 2007). The study found that mentor programs were quite diverse in their structure and focus. Big Brothers Big Sisters school-based mentoring program was neither a tutoring program nor a community-based mentor program placed inside the school. Instead the programs focused on the relationship development between mentor and mentee. Additionally many of the mentoring programs were reaching students with several risk factors and attracting a diverse group of volunteers. The programs were focused on schools in low-income areas that were facing challenges in meeting academic performance standards. In addition, the programs used teacher recommendations to identify students for the program. Eighty percent of the students who participated in the study received free or reduced-priced lunch and/or living in a single parent home (Herrera, Grossman Baldwin, Kauh, Feldman, & McMaken, 2007). Seventy–seven percent were struggling in one or more of four assessed areas of risk; this included academic performance, discipline, relationships and peer-reported misconduct.

The students involved received five months of school based mentoring during the first year of participation. At year's end the program had improved mentees' performance in many areas such as academic attitudes, performance and behaviors (Herrera, Grossman Baldwin, Kauh, Feldman, & McMaken, 2007). It was documented that the overall academic performance improved for mentees, as well as in the specific subjects of science, written and oral language, the quality of work, increase in homework performed and a decrease in discipline issues per mentee. The study also reported that scholastic efficacy increased a decrease in the number of unexcused absences (skipping). Mentees were also more willing to discuss personal issues as they relate to the lack of parental involvement. However, the study noted there were no out of school benefits as related to drugs, alcohol use, misconduct outside of school and community relationships (Herrera, Grossman Baldwin, Kauh, Feldman, & McMaken, 2007).

The study also noted that one year of intervention (mentoring) was not enough to permanently improve youth's academic performance (Herrera, Grossman Baldwin, Kauh, Feldman, & McMaken, 2007). The study further indicated that many of the mentees transferred during the second year of implementation of the program. According to the study this is typical of programs that serve the transition grade levels (fifth and eighth grades) (Herrera, Grossman Baldwin, Kauh, Feldman, & McMaken, 2007). Another factor having a significant impact on the study was the high attrition rate of the mentees involved. Mentees who did not participate in the second year of the program did not retain their positive school-related impacts at the second follow-up, supporting short term promote do not have permanent changes in behaviors.

Longer mentor mentee relationships were associated with stronger impacts. This was clearly demonstrated in the second year of the study by students who participated in year one and two of the program. Students who participated both years did better than their peers who did not participate after year one, this was evidenced by the classroom behavior and relationship with their teachers (Herrera, Grossman Baldwin, Kauh,

Feldman, & McMaken, 2007). The statistically significant difference between the two groups reinforced that the match between the length and relationship quality were important (Herrera, Grossman Baldwin, Kauh, Feldman, & McMaken, 2007).

Summer meetings between the mentees and mentors appeared to be important in the length and strength of the relationship. Another key to the success of the mentoring program mentioned in this study was the commitment level of school leaders to the program. Training and supervision of school based mentor programs was also key for the relationship between mentor and mentee. The study also revealed that school based mentor programs can operate with low cost, which averaged approximately $1000.00 a year (Herrera, Grossman Baldwin, Kauh, Feldman, & McMaken, 2007).

Making the Grade

The U.S. Department of Education published *Making the Grade*, which is a guide for organizations to incorporate academic achievement into mentoring programs (Cannata, Garringer, MacRae, & Wakeland, 2005). The guide highlights research studies which address peer mentoring, Big Brothers Big Sisters mentoring, elderly mentoring, and college student mentoring. According to the publication these are eight steps in the development of a successful mentoring program, they are the following: youth intake, volunteer recruitment, pre-match orientation and training, making the match, providing and encouraging appropriate mentoring activities, supervision and support, program evaluation, and staff roles and responsibilities (Cannata, Garringer, MacRae, & Wakeland, 2005). The Mentoring Resource Center provides a guide to the effective implementation of mentoring programs (Cannata, Garringer, MacRae, & Wakeland, 2005). Mentoring Resource center suggest when beginning a mentoring programs organizations should start with the "what" and then address the how. The "what" should focus on the impact that youth mentoring has on academic performance. The "how" explains the steps that were taken to effectively start and maintain the mentoring program. Another key aspect of creating an effective mentoring program is to clearly articulate the criteria for youth who participate in the program (Cannata, Garringer, MacRae, & Wakeland, 2005).

Establishing clear criteria for youth participating in the mentoring program is essential to the success of the program (Cannata, Garringer, MacRae, & Wakeland, 2005). Data must be gathered by the stakeholders involved in the youths' life. These data may include, but are not limited, to teachers, counselors, and parents. Pertinent information regarding the youths' grades, testing information, disciplinary or behavior, attitude toward school and educational/career interest must be collected (Cannata, Garringer, MacRae, & Wakeland, 2005). Another important piece of data may be academic areas of need for the youth such as test-taking skills, effective study habits. Other data should include information specific for certain youth such as rational numbers or geography. Making the grade emphasize collecting as much data as needed to really know youth and their needs (Cannata, Garringer, MacRae, & Wakeland, 2005). The information is invaluable when pairing youth with an appropriate mentor. Having the appropriate number of mentors requires a consistent recruitment effort on the part of the mentoring agencies.

Recruitment of volunteers should be based upon the majority need of the youth being mentored. For example if there were 20 youth interested in going into medicine then recruitment would center around medical professionals who are willing to volunteer.

The guide also points out the importance of broadening the students' horizons and exposing them to various careers. The most important factor in the recruitment of volunteers is to select persons who are consistent, supportive and committed to their mentoring responsibilities (Cannata, Garringer, MacRae, & Wakeland, 2005).

The guide clearly states the importance of training the mentors prior to pairing them with their mentees. It also emphasizes the importance of getting parents involved in the mentor and mentee relationship from the beginning. Supportive parents can make the relationship between mentor and mentee much easier and also important to academic achievement (Cannata, Garringer, MacRae, & Wakeland, 2005). Parents will have to provide consent for the minor child to have a mentor. The guidelines for mentors and mentees must be clear when discussing school and schoolwork. It is the responsibility of the mentor to assist the mentee to grow as a person and provide them with support, not to "fix" them or make them feel bad (Cannata, Garringer, MacRae, & Wakeland, 2005). Providing continuous responsive training gives everyone involved the skills to help the youth succeed academically (Cannata, Garringer, MacRae, & Wakeland, 2005).

Identifying the appropriate mentor and mentee pairing is key to making the program successful. The guide suggests identifying common interest and hobbies in making the matches. Certain academic considerations must also be factored in to the matching because that is the goal of the program. The program will need to decide how targeted it wants your matching strategy should be and to what point do academic needs outweigh personality and compatibility needs of a mentee.

The activities that mentors and mentees actively participate in should encourage strong relationships and bonds in a developmental context (Cannata, Garringer, MacRae,

& Wakeland, 2005). These activities should be carried out during the summer months as well to assist in the connectivity between the mentee and mentor. The guide list specific activities to maintain contact in the off-school months they are the following:

"Address and stamp five envelopes and ask the mentee to write to the mentor (a letter or drawing or a poem). Give your mentees little notebooks to record their summer activities to relate to their mentor when they see each other again, schedule a basketball or softball game among mentors and mentees, encourage matches to take an approved field trip to a local college to visit the campus, learn about courses, residence and financial aid, if you are in summer school, invite the mentors to visit them there for their mentoring, club activities and practices for fall football, band, and orchestra…." (Cannata, Garringer, MacRae, & Wakeland, 2005).

Supervision and support are necessary to monitor mentee and mentor relationships. Persons monitoring the program must check in often with mentors, youth, parents/guardians, teachers, counselors, and other stakeholders. The guide provides possible questions to ask youth that would allow for a view of the relationship between mentor and mentee. Checking in with mentors allows for a progression toward academic goals and quantitative information on the youth's attitudes, behaviors, and scholastic confidence (Cannata, Garringer, MacRae, & Wakeland, 2005). Monitoring parents' feelings toward the progress of the mentoring relationship is important in developing a positive relationship with the students. The parents can provide direct feedback on the progress of youth (Cannata, Garringer, MacRae, & Wakeland, 2005). Parents can also encourage youth to continue to participate in the program.

To effectively evaluate the program appropriate data must be collected. Grades, test scores, attendance data, and disciplinary referrals are among the types of necessary data to name a few (Cannata, Garringer, MacRae, & Wakeland, 2005). The guide also suggests the collection of quantitative data is as essential as quantitative data, as it helps the program to continue. Regular check–ins are also recommended to make sure matches are happy and progressing in a positive direction.

The key function for staff is the managerial role for mentoring programs. The key is to facilitate a connection to additional learning opportunities. In order for the programs to be successful, staff members must have a clear understanding of their role to effectively coordinate service work and opportunities for students. The match coordinators are essential, according to the guide, to monitor the matches. Match coordinators work closely to pair students with the appropriate mentors. The number of matches should not exceed 30 to 40, this allows for effective monitoring and feed back to mentors. Adequate staffing is essential to effectively monitor the program and maintain high quality. In chapter 3 the research will discuss the methodology, analysis of findings and instrumentation.

CHAPTER 3: RESEARCH DESIGN AND METHODOLOGY

Introduction

This chapter describes the research design and methods used to collect and analyze the research data from the present study, the other was designed to assess high school students' academic achievement, end-of-course test scores in Algebra I and English I to determine the effect of extended day learning programs and mentoring on students' academic performance. This study's research design and methodology expands previous research, which solely focuses on mentoring, by analyzing the effects on extended learning and mentoring on students' academic performance. This chapter discusses how the researcher analyzed the data. The following topics are discussed: (1) type of research methodology (2) sample and population, (3) instrumentation, (4) data collection procedures, (5) statistical analysis, (6) limitations, and (7) delimitations.

Overview of Study's Methodology

This study employed a quasi-experimental matched comparison group design in which a total of 232 Algebra I and English I students, were given the opportunity to participate in the intervention, which included an afterschool component, an extended day tutorial, and assigned mentors. The use of the quasi-experimental matched comparison group design allowed the researcher to determine if there were significant differences between Group A (treatment group, $n = 82$) students who were assigned mentors and participated in the afterschool extended day tutorial and Group B (control group, $n = 150$) students who did not participate in the after school extended day tutorial or have assigned mentors. Matched comparison group design was used because it allowed for comparison between two groups, one which received a treatment and another group with similarity with the treatment group, but did not receive the treatment. The students from both groups met the same criteria allowing extraneous influences to be minimized, by eliminating any advantages to either group. The students selected for the comparison and the treatment groups were all identified as bubble students. Bubble students had to meet the following criteria: those who scored a level III (on grade level) who fell three scale score points above or below the minimum a level III score. These students were highlighted because without any intervention they could have potentially not demonstrated grade level performance in within a year's time, even though they were only a few points from meeting the scoring criteria for level III.

A total of eighty-two students were selected in Algebra I and English I who participated in the afterschool extended day tutorials and were assigned mentors. The students were selected based upon the bubble criteria and their performances on their first semester exams and teacher recommendations. Both groups were given the pre-test, which was comprised of the same, algebra I and English I, eighth grade end of grade test for reading and mathematics that were used to classify the students for potential inclusion in the study and the post-test, which was the state required end of course test in algebra I and English I.

The majority of the students in the study were not on the appropriate grade level and were identified by the school's principal for intervention to bring their scores from a level II (not passing/not proficient) to a level three (passing/proficient). Most of the students in the program were not involved in any afterschool activity. In addition to scoring a level II or III on the practice test, descriptive cards were done on each participant to determine if attendance, discipline, or lack of motivation were possible reasons for not passing the practice test (see Appendix B student information card). In addition to the descriptive card a borderline information card was completed on each student. The border line information card showed student absences, suspensions, discipline referrals, and extracurricular activities. The cards were used to provide information to staff members who volunteered to become mentors for the students, in order to optimally benefit the students.

The mentors were staff members who volunteered to monitor bubble students Staff mentors included twenty-eight staff members, with each having at least five mentees. There were twenty female mentors and eight male mentors who actively participated. Mentors met with mentees on a weekly basis, ensured students attended extended day tutorial, met weekly with students and had bi-weekly contact with parents. Mentors also met as a group to discuss difficulties or success with their mentees. During these meetings mentors exchanged ideas on how to assist mentees through motivation, called meetings and casual meeting with their mentee. The mentors were required to keep documentation of all contact on their personal interest sheet. The sheet would identify the method of contact, date, time and a brief summary of their discussion with the parent, teacher(s), and student (mentee). Mentor meetings occurred in lieu of weekly staff meetings. These meetings were conducted for eighteen weeks, during the second semester. Students in the control group participated in the extended day program immediately after school on the school's campus.

Purpose Statement

The purpose of this study was to determine if there was a significant difference in the pretest scores of Algebra I and English I students in a regular education program who participated in the extended day program with an assigned mentor and students in regular education program who did not participate in the extended day and did not have the assistance of an assigned mentor.

There are two research questions that this study examines:

1. Is there a higher success rate on the end of course test in Algebra I and English I for the students who participated in the extended learning program and who had a mentor over the second semester?

2. Is there a significant difference in the performance rate of the end-of-course test scores in Algebra I and English I for those students in a regular education program who participated in the extended learning program and had a mentor as opposed to those who did not participate in an extended learning program and who did not have a mentor?

This study used a quasi-experimental matched comparison design which includes a control group and a non-control group, treatment group (Suter, 1998). Consistent with quasi-experimental matched comparison studies, this study was not a true experimental study, thus participants were not randomly selected to be in the treatment vs. baseline/control group (Suter, 1998). However, as Suter (1998) indicated, participants in the present study were matched according to the bubble criteria set forth by the district, which he argues is the next best thing to random assignment in experimental designs. The key to a successful quasi-experimental design is to have a well conceived matching design that can approximate the level of control provided by random assignments (Suter, 1998). Suter (1998) insists that this type of matching involves the selection of a comparison group (or individual subject) that is similar to the treatment group on one or more important variables that have a bearing on performance (the matched variables).

The students in this study all scored a level II, which denotes students who failed their end of grade test in the previous school year and were three scale points away from scoring a level III, which indicates passing the standardized test from the previous school year, on their prerequisite course. A student who scored a level III or better would be considered on grade level within the specified course (algebra or English I).

Validity was not compromised because the researcher was able to keep extraneous influences controlled through matching based on pre-requisite test scores (Suter, 1998). External validity, which refers to generalization, supports the quasi-experimental design of this study. The groups selected were representative of the larger student body population and the freshman class. The groups were also reflective of students who demonstrated the characteristics of freshmen in high schools. In addition to generalization to ninth grade students, it may also be generalized to a school that has a large population of African American students and low socioeconomic status. The design follows:

Matched Comparison Control Group Design

Matched (M)   Treatment (T)   Non-Control Group(NCG)   Posttest

Matched (M)   Control (C)   Control Group (CG)   Posttest

For this study, prerequisite score and the end of course score for the treatment group and the control group represented the matched variable.

The Bubble Students was the selected treatment group for the present study. The Bubble Students consisted of ninth grade students enrolled in Algebra I and English I who scored a level two on the pre-test for their enrolled course. The Bubble group consisted of 232 students in Algebra I and English I. From this group, the school's administration selected students who would be assigned mentors and participate in the extended learning program. For the purpose of this study, the group which was assigned mentors and selected to participate in the extended learning program will be called Group A, which is the control group. The remaining students were placed in Group B, which did not have any treatments applied to them. Each of the groups' participants completed the Algebra I and English I end of course tests.

Hypothesis

Students who attend a school based extended learning program and participate in a school based mentoring program will exhibit a one scale score increase or greater on the end of course tests.

Null Hypotheses

1. For students who received the treatment, there will be no statistically significant differences in academic performance on the end-of-course test.
2. For students who received the treatment, there will be no statistically significant difference in performance on the end of course test.

The level of statistical significance was set at $p < .05$. The researcher set this level to reduce the likelihood of committing a Type I or II error. Type I errors occur when a researcher mistakenly rejects the null hypothesis and concludes there is a relationship in the population when, in fact, there is not (Suter, 1998). Type II errors occur when the researcher wrongly accepts the null hypothesis and incorrectly concludes that there is no relationship in the population (Suter, 1998).

Sample Selection

In February of 2005, students from a school in the Southeastern United States were identified as scoring level II on the Algebra I and English I end-of-course pre-tests. This group of students became known as "being on the bubble" for academic success in the core subjects of Algebra I and English I. This identification was based on first and second quarter test results. In an effort to improve these scores, students were placed on teams that provided additional academic assistance and monitored school attendance; Group A students were assigned a mentor and were assigned to an after school extended learning program and mentoring programs. Group B students were bubble students were not required to participate in the mentoring program or extended learning program.

The researcher worked in conjunction with the school's principal to develop the program. The school's principal agreed to allow the researcher to analyze the data with the understanding that the identities of the students involved in the program would remain confidential. The school's testing facilitator, dropout prevention coordinator, and school administration collected student information and provided it to the researcher. Collected data were kept secure in a locked cabinet.

The scores on each of the tests would impact the Adequate Yearly Progress (AYP) of the school and the school's ABC's goals as set by the North Carolina Board of

Education. This information was provided by Student Performance At-Real Time Accessibility (SPARTA), a data resource for school administrators provided by the local school system and state.

The students selected to participate in the Bubble Program met three requirements:

1. They earned a score of two to four scale points above or below the range of the highest passing scale score on the prerequisite end of course test in Algebra I and/or English I.
2. They earned a pass/fail score on the current semester Algebra I and/or English I end of course exams by two to three scale points.
3. They received the recommendation of their Algebra I and/or English I teachers.

Various stakeholders at the school level provided information regarding these three requirements. The central office personnel provided the data for the first requirement regarding the prerequisite course information for all of the students who would qualify for the Bubble Program. The second criterion was determined using an analysis completed by the school's testing coordinator and school principal to determine pass/fail scale scores of central office Bubble students, who were the students Central Office identified as having earned 2 – 3 scale points above or below the passing scale score. Teachers and administrators completed the third requirement during their weekly team meetings. All of these requirements were put into place to impact student achievement. This selection of participants was similar to the selection criteria discussed by Suter (1998). Suter (1998) asserted that when selecting participants for quasi-experimental matched comparison design studies, is important that the researcher focus on the common variables (like characteristics) of both groups under comparison.

Common variables between the control and non-control group the level of academic achievement on the prerequisite test, 9th grade students and all enrolled in Algebra I and English I.

Meeting Student Needs

To meet the needs of each student, teams were developed for both algebra I and English I. The teams consisted of counselors, teachers, and administrative staff. Using this team approach, members of the teams selected students they would mentor. The team members selected students whom they had personal or content knowledge about to mentor. To assist teachers with more information about their selected mentees a card which identified the following information for each mentee was provided for each mentor: academic areas of focus, mentee participation in extracurricular activities, attendance, behavior contract, and current interventions students were currently involved.

The teachers also selected classes that were available during their planning period to act as classroom assistants for at least forty-five minutes at the beginning or end of the class period. The purpose for teachers assisting in the Algebra I and English I classes, was to provide students with one on one help during each class period during the eighteen week intervention. The identified students and their mentors became part of what was called the Bubble Program. The participants in the program were identified and monitored by administrative personnel and counselors. The students participated in the Bubble Program during the second semester.

The control group also consisted of students who failed their first and second quarter exams by scoring a level II which denotes students who scored in the not on grade level or not passing range and not scoring a level III, which denotes students who scored in the on grade level or passing range by two to four scale points. The control group contained 84 Algebra I students and 210 English I students who participated in the Bubble Program. Many of the students involved in the Bubble Program were enrolled in more than one course and, therefore, took more than one test.

Students in Group A received three interventions. Algebra I and English teachers were provided a team of nine teachers who volunteered their time. During this volunteer time teachers would go to classrooms and assist teachers during class. Both Groups A and B were selected based upon their pass/fail rates on the end of grade test. Students in Group A (treatment group) were provided the opportunity to receive extended learning four hours a week, two days each week and were also provided mentors. Students in Group B (control group) were given someone to monitor attendance, behavior, and provided an additional teacher in their English I and Algebra I classes.

Teacher mentors working with Group A maintained personal interest records (Appendix A) for each student and sent a letter of interest to parents (Appendix B). Parent letters were sent to inform parents that their children were involved in the bubble program and teacher mentors were given information about their mentees. Teachers met with students and content area colleagues once a week in lieu of weekly staff meetings. Teachers maintained weekly contact with parents to keep them abreast of various activities and student progress.

Instrumentation

The instrumentation used in this study was the North Carolina end of grade test for each course included in the Bubble Program. This state administered test, which all students are required to take, necessitates that students be tested under rigid conditions.

The test accounts for a significant proportion of students' final grades. For example, in the school system studied, the end of course test accounted for approximately 25% of the students' final grades. Teachers who administer this test are required to complete training prior to administering the test. If teachers do not follow the scripted guidelines provided by the state, the test is considered to be mis-administerd and the students have to take different forms of the test administered by other trained teachers. The North Carolina Department of Public Instruction (NCDPI) states in Technical Report 1: "The value of these tests lies primarily in the fact that the scores provide a common yardstick that is not influenced by local differences," which provides more validity to the test and its administration (Sanford, 1996). The test questions are based on Robert Marzano's Dimensions of Thinking (Sanford, 1996).

All students are given the same amount of time to complete the end-of-course tests. Test administrators are not allowed to assist students in any way that deviates from the scripted guidelines provided by the state. Only students who are currently under an Individualized Education Plan (IEP) or those who have a 504 (legal accommodations for students for a short term) in place that outlines specific academic accommodations are allowed extended time, modified materials, or directions that are read aloud.

Data Analysis

In quantitative research, there are various ways a researcher can analyze data. One way that many researchers have analyzed data is through a simple t-test. According to Suter (1998), quantitative data analysis using a simple t-test is the best test when comparing two matched comparison groups, a scenario where the researcher has two similar groups and a treatment is applied to one group only and both groups receive the same post-test. From the simple t-test, the researcher can determine the mean, standard deviation, and p-value of each group. A t-test is most commonly used to determine a significant difference between the means of two groups (Gay, 1996).

Upon receiving the information, the researcher sorted the data and organized it by subject area. In order to preserve the anonymity of the students, there no references were made about individual student achievements but only as group achievements, which were referenced by course only.

The school district, school administration, and the students' classroom teachers identified the students selected to participate in the program. The students' scores were examined to determine if a difference occurred between students' practice assessment and their end of course test. Their performance was at grade level (level 3 or better) or not at grade level (level 2 or less). The scores were placed in a Microsoft Excel data base for English I and Algebra I. The differences between the semester exam and the end of course test were determined, and the number of students increasing by 10 or more scale points was calculated for each subgroup (Algebra I and English I). The total number of students with less than a 10-point gain was also calculated. A one-sample t-test was used to determine if there were significant differences between the scores of the students who participated in the program compared to the students who did not.

Limitations

This study has the following limitations:

    a. The length of time for interventions, attendance of the students and level of involvement of each mentor. The interventions were lasted eight weeks and students year long daily attendance varied by student.

    b. The same teacher did not teach all of the students, and some students were taught by as many as four instructors throughout the school year.

    c. Since the study was a quasi-experimental matched comparison design, participants were not randomly assigned to the two groups.

    d. The data are only available to publish in group form.

The findings of this research were limited by several factors. The nature of the quasi-experimental design did not allow the researcher to randomly assign participants to either of the groups. Consequently, the independent variable could not be manipulated because it had already been predetermined. Another limitation was related to the sample size. The study did not include a sample of all students in a large urban district; it included a sample of students from only one high school with a population between 1200–1500 students. This restriction meant that the findings of the study could only be generalized to schools that have a similar size and demographic composition.

Additionally, not all students who were designated by the district participated in the program. The exact student group who met the criteria to participate in the Bubble Program and participated were not able to be placed in the program the following year due to the transitional nature of the urban district and their academic success on the end of course test.

Delimitations

This study has the following delimitations:

    a. The study involved 232 students from each of the following courses: Algebra I and English I classes who scored one or two points above or below the scale score to pass their End of Course Test on their previous End of Grade Test.

b. These students were identified as students on the bubble by the school system's central office personnel, based upon their pre-requisite courses during the previous school year.

c. There were 232 students identified by their Algebra I and English I teachers based upon their performance on the Algebra I, and English I quarterly exams and recommended for interventions.

d. The identified students could have passed their end-of-course exams with appropriate interventions.

e. The following interventions were implemented: Mentors (teachers from content areas (Algebra I and English I) and non-content (elective classes), Afterschool Extended Day Tutorial, and parental contact.

Summary

Chapter III presented the type of research utilized in this study, a quasi-experimental matched comparison group design. The populations of students were the same for the non-control group and the control group, which increased the validity of the study because there was not a random assignment to each group (Suter, 1998). Data was collected at the beginning of the year on students' pre-tests for Algebra I and English I, at mid-year, and again at the end of the year (Gay, 1996). The data collection identified students for The Bubble Program and demonstrated the on grade level performance rate of students. A simple t-test was performed which compared the two groups' performance rates and means on the end of course test.

This study was conducted in an urban high school in the southeastern part of the United States. The end of course test determined their performance was at grade level (level 3 or better) or not at grade level (level 2 or less). A descriptive and quasi-experimental matched comparison grouped design was employed. The data were collected using the results of the North Carolina end-of-course for each subject area.

CHAPTER 4: RESULTS

Introduction

The purpose of this study was to determine the effects of mentoring and extended day programs on students' performance on the North Carolina English I and Algebra I end of course test. The research examined the effects of students receiving mentors within the school building to monitor academic performance on end of course test. This research will assist educators seeking interventions for struggling high school students in Algebra I and English I to potentially increase classroom and standardized test performance. The study analyzes student academic performance on the Algebra I and English I when students participate in mentoring and extended learning programs. In this chapter we will discuss what the results were after the treatment.

The research design used was quasi-experimental matched comparison group design. This design allowed the researcher to maximize the already intact groups, identified as bubble students. The design also allowed the researcher to ensure validity was not compromised. Based on the selected design extraneous influences were minimized through matching (Suter, 1998). External validity, which refers to generalization, supports the quasi-experimental design of this study. The bubble students were representative of the school general freshman class. Bubble students were also reflective of typical high school students across the nation. Bubble students in addition to generalization to ninth grade students, can also be generalized to a school that has a large population of African American students and low socioeconomic status. The design follows:

Matched Comparison Control Group Design

Matched (M)   Treatment (T) Non-Control Group (NCG)   Posttest

Matched (M)   Control (C)   Control Group (CG)   Posttest

For this study, the bubble students, practice test and the end-of-course score for the treatment group and the control group represented the matched variables.

The Bubble Program was the selected treatment for the present study. Subjects consisted of ninth grade students enrolled in Algebra I and English I who scored a level two on the pre-test for their enrolled course. The Bubble group consisted of 232 students in Algebra I and English I. From this group, the school's administration selected students who would be assigned mentors and participate in the extended learning program. For the purpose of this study, the group which was assigned mentors and selected to participate in the extended learning program will be called Group A, which is the control group. The remaining students were placed in Group B, which did not have any treatments applied to them. Each of the groups' participants completed the Algebra I and English I end of course tests.

Prior to the end of course test (second semester) students were placed in the bubble program based on their previous year's end of grade test. Once the students were identified, attendance, behavior, and content course grades reviewed, the school placed the students' names on a list for teachers to select who they would be willing to mentor.

When the selections were made teachers were provide with the student information cards, a sample parent letter, personal interest sheet, and a copy of the students' schedule. Each mentor was required to meet with the student's weekly, contact parents bi-weekly and contact the student's core subject teachers. The mentors were required to keep documentation of all contact on their personal interest sheet, that was provided by the administration (Appendix B). The sheet would identify the method of contact, date, time and a brief summary of their discussion with the parent, teacher(s), and student (mentee).

Hypothesis

Students who attend a school based extended learning program and participate in a school based mentoring program will exhibit a one scale score increase or greater on the end of course tests.

Null Hypotheses

1. For students who received the treatment, there will be no statistically significant differences in academic performance on the end of course test.

2. For students who received the treatment, there will be no statistically significant difference in grade level performance on the end of course test.

Sample Description

The school's principal and the researcher selected participants from all students who were identified as "Bubble Students" for passing their end of course test and also assigned the control group case managers (mentors) who were required to meet with the students on a weekly basis. The mentors were staff members, who came from various ethnic backgrounds (Asian, African-American, Caucasian, African, Indian and Asian), were required by the building principal to select specific students who were "Bubble Students" to mentor.

A total of 232 students were identified as on the bubble students. Eighty-two students (34.6%) were in the non-control group. Of the participants in the control group, 40 (48.8%) were male and 42 (51.2%) were female (See Table 1). The remaining bubble students were the control group, which consisted of 66 (44%) males and 84 (56%) females (See Table 1).

Table 1

Gender of Bubble Students Control and Non-Control Groups

Gender	Total N	%	Non-Control Group N	%	Control Group N	%
Male	106	45.7	40	48.8	66	44
Female	126	54.3	42	51.2	84	56

Table 2 provides more descriptive information about the participants. The racial background of the participants is as follows: 204 (87.9%) were African-American, 20 (8.6%) were White, 5 (2.1%) were Hispanic, 2 (0.86%) were Asian, and 1 (0.43%) was Other. The ethnic make-up of the non-control group consisted of 80 (97.6%) African-Americans, 2 Asians (2.4%) and 10 Caucasian. Table two depicts this information:

Table 2

Reported Ethnicity of Student in Each School Group

Ethnicity	N	%	NCG	CG
African –American	204	87.9	80	124
White	20	8.6	10	10
Hispanic	5	2.1		5
Asian	2	.86	2	0
Other	1	.43		1
Total	232	100%	92	140

The participants in the control group (NCG) end of course pre-test mean score for English I was 40.9 (*mdn* = 41.6, *SD* = 5.00). The mean English I pre-test end-of-course score for participants in the control group (CG) was 45 (*mdn* = 46.5, *SD* = 4.20). A t-test was performed, which compared the mean English I end-of-course scores between the two groups and revealed a statistically significant difference between the two groups ($t = 5.9436$, $p < .05$). The mean Algebra I pre-test end of grade score for participants in the non-control group was 37 (*mdn* = 38.5, *SD* = 5.00). The mean Algebra I pre-testend of course score for participants in the non-control group was 39 (*mdn* = 39.8, *SD* = 7.0). A t-test was performed, which compared the mean Algebra I pre-test end-of -course scores between the two groups ($t = 1.5171$, $p < .05$). The simple t-test was conducted to determine if the grade level performance rate between the two groups were not statistically significant for Algebra I. These results can be viewed below in Table 3.

Table 3

Sample Sizes, Means, Standard Deviation, Median for Control Group and Non-Control Group Practice end-of-course test data (Algebra I and English I)

		CG				NCG		
Practice Test	N	Median	M	SD	N	Median	M	SD
English I	125[a]	45.5	45	4.20	85[a]	52.9	40.9	5.50
Algebra I	44[a]	53.00	37.0	5.02	40[a]	52.0	39.0	7.30

Note. [a] indicates the sample size decreased due to participants leaving the school.

The participants in the control group (NCG) end-of-course mean score for English I was 55.4 (*mdn* = 55.5, *SD* = 4.80). The mean English I end-of-course score for participants in the control group (CG) was 52.9 (*mdn* = 53.5, *SD* = 5.06). A t-test was performed, which compared the mean English I end-of-course scores between the two groups and revealed a statistically significant difference between the two groups (*t* =3.6242 , *p* < .05).The mean Algebra I end of grade score for participants in the non-control group was 53.4 (*mdn* = 53.0, *SD* = 6.21). The mean Algebra I end-of-course score for participants in the non-control group was 51.9 (*mdn* = 52.0, *SD* = 8.30). A t-test was performed, which compared the mean Algebra I end-of-course scores between the two groups (*t* = .9432, *p* < .05). The simple t-test was conducted to determine if the grade level performance rate between the two groups were not statistically significant for Algebra I. These results can be viewed below in Table 4.

Table 4

Sample Sizes, Means, Standard Deviation, Median for Control Group and Non-Control Group end-of-course Test Scores (English I and Algebra I)

		CG				NCG		
end-of-course test	N	Median	M	SD	N	Median	M	SD
English I	125[a]	55.5	55.4	4.80	85[a]	52.9	52.9	5.06
Algebra I	44[a]	53.00	53.4	6.21	40[a]	52.0	51.9	8.30

Note. [a] indicates the sample size decreased due to participants leaving the school.

T-tests demonstrated there was no statistical significant difference between the two groups for the English I end-of-course test ($t = 3.3158, p < .05$). There was a difference in student average between the control group and non-control group. The median for the control group was 8.00, the mean was 9.62, and the standard deviation was 8.21. The median for the non-control group was 13.0, the mean was 13.8, and the standard deviation was 9.98. The t-test was conducted to determine if the grade level performance rate between the two groups were statistically significant for English I. See Table 5 for complete details.

Table 5

Growth Comparison For Practice Test and End-Of-Course Comparison English I

end-of-course test	N	Median	Mean	SD
Control Group	125[a]	8.00	9.62	8.21
Non-Control Group	85[a]	13.00	13.8	9.98

Note. [a] indicates the sample size decreased due to participants leaving the school.

The researcher also examined if there was a significant difference in the mean grade level performance between the non-control group and the control group for Algebra

I. There was no statistically significant difference between the two groups on the Algebra I end of course test. A t-test conducted on the differences between the third quarter end of course practice test and the final test score demonstrated the lack of a statistical difference ($t = 1.191$, $p < .05$).

The median for the non-control group was 16.0, mean was 15.3 and the standard deviation was 8.36. The median for the control group was 12.0, the mean was 13.00 and the standard deviation was 9.34. The simple t-test was conducted to determine if the grade level performance rate between the two groups was not statistically significant for Algebra I.

Table 6

Growth Comparison for Practice Test and End-Of-Course Algebra I

end-of-course test	N	Median	Mean	SD
Control Group	44[a]	16.00	15.30	8.36
Non-Control Group	40[a]	12.00	13.00	9.34

Note. [a] indicates the sample size decreased due to participants leaving the school.

The researcher analyzed the data and found that a Type II error may have occurred with the Algebra I mean (Table 2) sample. A Type II error may have occurred due to the over representation of the level II students in the Algebra I mean (Table 2) sample. Due to the lack of random selection, this type of error is very possible (Suter, 1998). The sample was a matched comparison which is the next best thing to true randomization (Suter, 1998). This result then required the researcher to accept the null hypothesis for the non-control group for Algebra I based on a Type II error (beta error) again because of the over representation of level II. If the study is replicated, the researcher recommends that sample selection must allow for a more diverse levels be placed in the sample and a larger sample size for the Algebra I group.

The grade level performance mean (13) in the Algebra I NCG (Table 5) was less than the Control groups mean (15.3) however due to the number of level II students who were a part of the sample accounts for the difference in the pre-test means. This also suggests that when teachers selected this group they may have selected the students on the lower range as opposed to the students three scale score points above the level III. The control group's mean was less than the Algebra I non-control group. This result then required the researcher to accept the null hypothesis for the non-control group for Algebra I based on a Type II error (beta error) again because of the over representation of level II. It is important to note that Algebra I is the lowest level of college preparatory math offered at the high school level, which would also take into account for the lower pre-test mean for non-control group.

The mean (13.68) Table 4 in the English I Non-Control Group was more than the Control group's growth means (9.62) Table 4. The researcher was able to reject the null and found the hypothesis to be true. There was not a Type II error (beta error) due to the sample size for English I group and the sample did not have one group that was more representative than another. The researcher found this to be true due to the larger sample size for English I, which provided a wider range of level III's and level II's. In high school all students are required to take English I in the 9th grade. This means a larger number of students were able to be selected as bubble students and the comparison groups were able to be more random.

Chapter 4 included the presentation and analyses of data gained from the practice end-of-course and actual end-of-course test for Algebra I and English I. Chapter 4 also included data that compared the growth rate between Algebra I and English I. T-tests were performed to make comparisons of each control and non-control groups and to determine the probability of obtaining statistically significant results. Summary, conclusions and recommendations are presented in Chapter 5.

CHAPTER 5: CONCLUSION

This study examined the effects of mentoring and extended day programs on students' performance on end-of-course test. The school in present study utilized staff members as volunteer mentors and classroom teachers to instruct during the extended day program. The school's administration selected the participants based on their potential to increase grade level scores by one or more points.

Research Questions

The following research questions were examined:

1. What were the reported changes in the end of grade test in Algebra I, and English I for the students who participated in the extended learning program over the second semester?

2. Is there a significant difference in the growth end of grade test scores in Algebra I and English I for those students in a regular education program who participated in Extended Learning Program as opposed to those who did not participate in an Extended Learning Program?

To seek answers to these questions, quantitative data collection and analyses were utilized. The researcher compared the practice test of students at semester break to the end of course results at the end of the school year. The researcher took the results of 232 students of the entire group (85 were in the non-control group participated in the intervention, and 125 were in the control group and did not participate in the intervention).The test results were recorded in an excel spreadsheet, and were then put into a SPSS data system. T-tests were performed to compare the two groups' end of course test scores and the growth rate between the two groups in both Algebra I and English I.

Summary of Findings

This research study sought to find answers to the following research questions:

1. What were the reported changes in the end of course test in Algebra I and English I for the students who participated in the extended learning program over the second semester?

2. Is there a significant difference in the growth from the practice test to the actual end-of-course test scores in Algebra I and English I for those students in a regular education program who participated in Extended Learning Program as opposed to those who did not participate in an extended learning program?

In comparing the means of the end of course test for students the researcher found there was a statistically significant difference between the control group and non-control group on the English I test. This would then imply that the interventions put in place for the non-control group did have an effect on the means on the end of course test. This means for the researcher students who participated in the extended learning mentoring program were affected by the previously stated interventions (programs) and the results were not due to chance. In comparing the means of the end of course test for students on the Algebra I end of course test the researcher found that there was not a statistically significant difference between the means. This means for the researcher students who participated in the extended learning mentoring program were not affected by the previously stated interventions (programs) and the results may be due to chance.

In comparing the growth means for English I between the control group and the non-control group the researcher found that there was statistically significant difference between the means. This means for the researcher students who participated in the extended learning mentoring program were affected by the previously stated interventions (programs) and the results were not due to chance. In comparing the growth means for Algebra I between the control group and the non-control group the researcher found that there was not statistically significant difference between the means of the groups. This means for the researcher students who participated in the extended learning mentoring program may not have been affected by the previously stated interventions (programs) and the results may be due to chance.

Discussion

The researcher used the data analysis from the means of the control group and non-control group to answer the research questions that prompted the study. The key research questions and responses follow:

a. What were the reported changes in the end of course test in Algebra I, and English I for the students who participated in the extended learning program mentoring program over the second semester?

The average student scores on the English I end of course test were affected by the extended learning and mentoring program put in place by the school's administration. This indicates it would be to a high school's advantage to actively involve students in an extended learning and mentoring program at their schools. The means of the students were the non-control group were in the range at grade level range (50 and above), which means the average student who participated in the programs passed their end of course test by scoring a level III or level IV on their end of course test. The means of the students in Algebra I of the non-control group were in the at grade level range (45 and above), which means the average student who participated in the programs passed their end of course test.

b. What were the reported changes in the end of course test in Algebra I and English I for the students who did not participate in the extended learning and mentoring program?

The average English I student score in the control group were in the range at grade level range (50 and above), which means the average student who did not participate in the programs passed their end of course test by scoring a level III or level IV on their English I end of course test. The average Algebra I student score in the control group were in the range at grade level range (45 and above), which means the average student who did not participate in the programs passed their end of course test by scoring a level III or level IV on their Algebra I end of course test.

c. What were average growth rates between the practice test and end-of-course for Algebra and English I students who participated in the extended learning program?

When comparing the practice test scores to the actual test students demonstrated on average a 13.8 point growth on their English I end of course test. When comparing the practice test scores to the actual test students demonstrated an average 13.0 point gain on their Algebra I end of course test.

d. What were the reported changes in the growth for Algebra I and English I students who did not participate in the extended learning program and mentoring program?

When comparing the practice test scores to the actual test students demonstrated on average a 9.62 point growth on their English I end of course test. When comparing the practice test scores to the actual test students demonstrated an average 15.30 point gain on their Algebra I end of course test.

The results on the English I end of course test demonstrate that non-control group was impacted by the extended learning programs put in place. More significantly the growth rate of the English I non-control group was an average increase of 14 points from the practice test to the actual end-of-grade this is important for educators as the requirements for student growth become more stringent and teachers are held more accountable for student growth. With the growth model in place assisting students by offering these programs can only assist in the student's ability to grow within one academic school year. Educational leaders consider alternatives for high school students to provide them with a more successful high school experience.

The results on the Algebra I end of course test demonstrates that non-control group was not impacted however the students did demonstrate growth base on the mean of the growth between the practice test and actual end of course. The sample size of for Algebra I was significantly smaller than that of English I, this may have caused a Type II error to occur (Suter, 1998).

Implications

The work of previous researchers provided the importance of extended day programs and mentoring for youth. The improvement by students in the end of course testing demonstrates the effectiveness of the extended day program and mentoring. Researchers agree that extended day programs appear to have a positive effect on academic performance of students (TASC, 2001). Researchers report that the academic performance of middle school students who have mentors positively affected (TASC, 2001). In an examination of related literature such as Marva Collins, the researcher found evidence those students who had both a mentor and participated in the extended day program were more likely to increase by one and a half grade levels compared to their classmates who may or may not have seen an improvement in their end of course test scores.

The matched comparison research design used in this study allowed for the comparison of bubble students, and their practice and end-of-course test as the matched variables. Future research would need to considered more matched variables such as gender and ethnicity. These additional variables would provide for more comparison among the control and non-control groups. It would also allow a researcher explore the idea that Pajare and Bandura's self efficacy and academics.

Such authors as Marva Collins and Darling-Hammond published findings that demonstrated the importance of developing and maintaining mentor and extended learning programs for students. The results of the present study suggest a strong need for educators to give attention to content subject (English I and Algebra I) as the study indicates a significant increase in the passing rate on the end of course test scores for participating students. The researcher suggests a strong need for educators to actively seek opportunities to mentor students and participate in school based extended learning programs. Practices based on the foregoing indicators suggest schools that seek better performances on end of grade or end of course tests should implement mentoring and extended learning programs for students who have the potential to increase or decrease in their performance on these tests, thereby maximizing the use of staff that are within the school's community.

The researcher found that variation in the rate of change between the control group and non-control group places an emphasis on providing alternative resources to assist students in their academic achievement. The researcher recommends a continued development of mentor and extended learning programs that are specifically directed toward assisting students' academic performance. Classroom teachers must be informed of the significance of mentoring and extending learning on academic performance. Regardless of teachers' willingness to participate in extended learning programs, the researcher strongly believes that all teachers can mentor at least one two students within the schools community based on the individual student growth.

Recommendations

The researcher suggests that:

1. Schools require bubble students to participate in an extended learning program implemented by the school.
2. Schools train and assign teacher mentors to students who qualify for the program.

This analysis of differences among student academic performance levels in regard to end of course test ratings were descriptive in nature. The findings and limitations of this study have led to the researcher to make the following recommendations for further research:

1. Additional research needs to be conducted on mentoring program designs for high school students.
2. A study similar to the current one should be conducted with high school students who are continuously enrolled in extended learning programs through out their high school tenure.
3. There should be additional studies conducted on how to most effectively assess students' relationships with mentors as it relates to student achievement.

In the twenty-first century, public attention will continue to center on two themes in education. First, there is a need to help students obtain academic success globally because the school system and its practices will remain the highlight of media and political debates. The growing number of impoverished high school students failing within the public school system must be addressed within the schools available resources with minimal cost. This reinforces the need to utilize teachers (in-house) mentors and tutors to minimize the cost to local school districts. The need to assist students who come from low socioeconomic backgrounds by minimizing barriers that may prohibit their academic success addressed by directly connecting them to the school community and creating positive relationships through mentoring and extended day learning programs. The growth data supports the continuation of school based extended day learning programs at the high school level.

The second issue is connecting high school students to both their school's community and world wide community. As the second issue intensifies, educators must be prepared to develop key mentoring relationships with students to facilitate the connection between students and their school's community. Globally competitive education will foster the ability of educators to meet these challenges within their schools' communities. If clear guidelines are put in place for mentoring, there will be significant impacts on students' academic performances by the end of first semester. Schools must seek every opportunity to maximize the number of students impacted by both extended learning and mentoring programs. High schools must become geared toward promoting extended learning and mentoring programs. Until high schools begin to address both of these areas school systems will continue to under serve their students.

The previously stated studies have addressed extended day program and mentoring program and how they affect student progress in and out of school. When students are involved in extended learning programs and mentoring they benefit academically. School-based mentoring allows for closer monitoring, scholastic efficacy, decrease in discipline issues and improved academic performance. In the current study the application of both extended day program and mentoring were used together increase the probability of student success. Pajares' work focused on self-efficacy and its effects on different forms of assessment open ended, free response, and multiple choice. Pajares work pointed out that many students' confidence is over inflated regarding their ability to solve mathematics problems, thus creating lower test scores. Self-efficacy was addressed by two of mentoring studies through scholastic efficacy. The mentees belief regarding their ability to do better in school was enhanced when students were assigned a mentor. However, in each study the result was the same; self-efficacy had minimal effect on the students' actual performance on the test.

Many studies have been conducted on school-based extended learning and mentoring programs independently, however studies have not been done on the implementation of both extended learning and mentoring. This study has the potential to expand research in whole different direction and bring the focus of mentoring with extended learning opportunities collectively not as two distinct programs. It also has the potential to further research with teachers having a greater presence in students' lives beyond academics. Finally this research expands other research and can be replicated at the school level to help students meet requirements that will assist them in passing state mandated exams. The current study has the potential to act as a guide in helping schools to meet goals with the new pay for performance initiative that is currently sweeping the country. With schools being asked to do more with less the current study also provides the avenue for low cost mentoring and extended learning opportunities for schools.

REFERENCES

Ascher, C. (1991). The changing face of racial isolation and desegregation in urban schools. Retrieved June 19, 2002 from http://eric-web.tc.columbia.edu/diget/dig91.htm

Afterschool Alliance. (2002). Retrieved May 25, 2005 from http://www.afterschoolalliance.org/prop_49.cfm

Alexander, D. (2000). The learning that lies between play and academics in after-school programs. Wellesley, MA: National Institute on Out-of-School Time. Retrieved April, 2006 from http://www.noist.org/activitiy.html

Archer, J. (2006). NC judge's threat puts heat on high schools. Education news week. Retrieved May 05, 2006 from www.edweek.org/ew/articles/2006/03/22/28nc.h25.html

Baker, B. D., Keller-Wolff, C., & Wolf-Wendel, L. (2000). Two steps forward, one step back: Race/ethnicity and student achievement in education policy research. *Educational Policy, 14*, 19.

Banks, J. (1994). Transforming the mainstream curriculum. *Educational Leadership, 51*, 4-8.

Bugarin, R., Warburton, E. C., & Nunez A.-M. (2001). Bridging the gap: Academic preparation and postsecondary success of first-generation students. Education Statistics Quarterly, vol. 3 n. 3 p73-77. Fall 2001.

Bandura, A. (1986). *Social foundations of thought and action: A social cognitive theory.* Englewood Cliffs, NJ: Prentice Hall.

Caldas, S.J., & Banskston, C. (1997). Effects of school socioeconomic status on individual academic achievement. *Journal of Educational Research and Improvement,* 120 (5), 179 – 184)

Cannata, A., Garringer, M., MacRae, P., & Wakeland, D. (2005). *Making the Grade A Guide to Incorporating Acadmic Achievement into Mentoring Programs and Relationships.* folsom: U.S. Department of Education Mentoring Resource Center.

Coates, R.D., & Wagenaar, T. C. (2000). Race and children: The dynamics of early socialization. *Educational Research, 120*, 220 – 236.

Cole, R. W., Armento, B., Bafumo, M. E., Causey, V. F., Cohen, B., Cole, R. W., et al. (2001). *More strategies for educating everybody's children*. Retrieved April 2006 from http://www.ascd.org/readingroom/books/cole01book.html

Crosby, E. A. (1999). Urban schools: Forced to fail. *Phi Delta Kappan, 81*, 298 – 303.

Darling-Hammond, L. (1997). Structuring learner-centered schools. In *The right to learn: A blueprint for creating schools that work (pp. 1 - 379)*. San Francisco: Jossey-Bass.

Frazier, J.A., & Morrison, F.J. (1998). The influence of extended year schooling on growth and achievement and perceived competence in early elementary school. Child Development, v69 n2 p495-517 Apr 1998

Gibson, R. (2001). Bridging the gap: Whole language, inclusion, and critical social action. *The Rouge Forum, 3*, 6-10.

Green, R.S. (2001). Closing the achievement gap: Lessons learned and challenges ahead. *Teaching & Change, 8*, 215-225.

Grissmer, D., Flanagan, A., & Williamson, S. (1997). *Does money matter for minority and disadvantaged students? Assessing the new empirical evidence*. Retrieved November 2005 from http://nces.ed.gov/pubs98/dev9//98212a.html

Halpern, R. (1992). The role of after-school programs in the lives of inner-city children: A study of "urban youth network". *Child Welfare, 71*, 215-230.

Halpern, R. (2002). A different kind of child development institution: The history of after-school programs for low income children. *Teachers College Record, 104*, 178-211.

Hankes, J. (1996). An alternative to basic-skills remediation. *Teaching Children Mathematics, 2*, 452 – 458.

Herrera, C., Grossman Baldwin, J., Kauh, T. J., Feldman, A. F., & McMaken, J. (2007). *Making a Difference In Schools*. New York: Public Private Ventures.

Jucovy, L., & Garringer, M. (2007). *The ABCs of School Based Mentoring*. Portland: The Hamilton Fish Institute on School and Community Violence & The National Mentoring Center at Northwest Regional Educational Laboratory.

Kugler, M. (2001). The why and how of after-school programs. *Education Digest, 67*, 44 – 50.

Johnson, L. (2002). My eyes have been opened: White teachers and racial awareness. *Journal of Teacher Education, 53*, 153-168.

Khane, J., Nagaoka, J., Brown, A., O'Brien, J., Quinn, T., & Thiede, K. (2001). Assessing after school programs as contexts for youth development. Youth & Society, 32(4),421-46.

Ladson-Billings, G. (2001). They're supposed to learn something. In *Crossing over Canaan: The journey of new teachers in diverse classrooms.* Cochran- Smith, M. *(pp. 120-150).* San Francisco: Jossey-Bass.

Ladson, B. G. (1994). What we can learn from multicultural educational research. *Educational Leadership, 51*, 22-26.

National Association of State Boards of Education. (2002). A more perfect union. Retrieved July 5, 2002, from http://www.nasbe.org/NASBE_Bookstore/Covers/perfect_union.html.

National Coalition for the Homeless. (1999). *Education of homeless children and youth* (NCH Fact Sheet No 10). Retrieved November 2003from http://nch.ari.net/edchild.html

Navarro, M.S., & Natalico, D.S. (1999). Closing the achievement gap in El Paso. Phi Delta Kappan, 80(8), 597-601.

Nunez, R. (2001). Family homelessness in New York City: A case study. *Political Science Quarterly, 116*, 367-379.

Pajares, F. (1996). Self-Efficacy beliefs in academic settings. *Review of Educational Research*, 66 (4),543-78.

Peele, H. (1993). Cultural sensitivity in the young child's learning environment. *The Delta Kappa Gamma Bulletin, 60*, 21-25.

Pianta, R.C., La Paro, K.M., Payne, C., Cox, M.J., & Bradley, R. (2002). The relation of kindergarten classroom environment to teacher, family, and school characteristics and child outcomes. *The Elementary School Journal, 102*, 225-240.

Pilkington, A. (1999). Racism in schools and ethnic differentials in educational achievement: A brief comment on a recent debate. *British Journal of Sociology of Education, 20*, 411-417.

Posner, J., & Vandell, D. (1999). After-school activities and development of low-income urban children: A longitudinal study. *Developmental Psychology, 35*, 868-879.

Roach, R. (2001). Gaining new perspectives on the achievement gap. *Black Issues in Higher Education, 18*, 24-26.

Sanford, E. E. (1996). *Technical report #1: North Carolina end-of-grade tests.* Raleigh, NC Public Schools of North Carolina.

Schwartz, W. (2001) *Closing the achievement gap: Principles for improving the educational success of all students.* Retrieved October 2003. http://eric.web.tc.columbia.edu/digests/dig169.html

Scott-Little, C., Hamann, M.S., & Jurs, S. (2002). Evaluations of after-school programs: A meta-evaluation of methodologies and narrative synthesis of findings. *American Journal of Evaluation*, 23 (3), 387-419.

Shann, M.H. (2001). Students' use of time outside of school: A case for after school programs for urban middle school youth. *The Urban Review, 33(2)*, 339-356.

Shumow, L. (2001). Academic effects of after-school programs. Washington, D.C. Office of Educational Research and Improvement. ERIC Clearinghouse on Elementary and Early Childhood Education Champaign IL. ED458010.

Sipe, C. L. (1996). *Mentoring: A Synthesis of P/PV's Research.* Philadelphia: Public Private Ventures.

Slavin, R.E., & Maden, N. (2001). Reducing the gap: Success for all and the achievement of African-American and Latino Students. Washington, D.C. Office of Educational Research and Improvement. Retrieved February 2002. http://www.eric.ed.gov/ERICWebPortal/recordDetail?accno=ED455079

Tatum, B.D. (1999). *"Why are all the black kids sitting together in the cafeteria?" and other conversations about race.* New York: Basic Books.

Thompson, C., & Quinn, S. (2001). *First in America special report: Eliminating the black-white achievement gap.* Chapel Hill: North Carolina Education Research Council.

Vissing, Y. M. (1998). *Homeless children: Addressing the challenge in rural schools.* New York, NY: Teachers College.

APPENDIX A

Sample Parent Letter

*Date*_____

Dear Parent,

I have volunteered to serve as a mentor to your child _____ *in order that he/she might be successful on the End of Course tests.*

I will be talking to each student periodically, offering words of encouragement, checking their progress, and perhaps making some helpful suggestions where needed.

I am certain that you want the very best for your child. I would appreciate your signature and any comments that you would care to make regarding this matter. Please feel free to contact me should you have further questions or comment. My contact information is:

*Teacher Name*_____ *Phone: (555) 555-5555*

The success of our children is the most vitally important goal we will ever attain. Together we can make it happen.

Warm regards,

Teacher Name

Parent Name _____ Phone: _____

Parent Signature_____

APPENDIX B

_____High School
Mentoring Program

Teacher Name: _____ Student Name:_____

Based on discussion during the general faculty meeting of February ____, 200?, we have identified students who, with additional support, have the ability to succeed on the EOCs. Our objective through this program is for these students to achieve level III ore Level IV in June.

Listed above is the name of a student you have agreed to mentor for the remainder of the school year.

We will revisit this program through follow-up activities a future faculty meeting to address successes and concerns of our interaction with these students.

Action to be taken by Mentor

Contact with student   Date: _____ Time: _____
                                  Method of contact: _____
                                  Discussion: _____
                                  _____
                                  _____
                                  _____

Contact with parent   Date: _____ Time: _____
                                  Method of contact: _____
                                  Discussion: _____
                                  _____
                                  _____
                                  _____

Contact with subject teacher (s) Date: _____ Time: _____
                                  Method of contact: _____
                                  Discussion: _____
                                  _____
                                  _____
                                  _____

                                  Subject: _____

APPENDIX C

_____High School
Students on the Bubble

Name:_____ Student ID:_____

Behavior Concerns: _____
　　　　　　　　　　_____
　　　　　　　　　　_____

Attendance (days absent) _____

Interventions

Student Academic Behavior Contract _____ yes (Date of Contract) _____ _____no

Extended Day: ____Yes (Date of Enrollment)　　　　　　　　　　_____no

Core Academy:_____ Yes (Course Currently Enrolled)　　　　　_____no

Teacher Mentor _____

CPSIA information can be obtained
at www.ICGtesting.com
Printed in the USA
LVIC06n1557090114
368765LV00017B/73